THERE WILL ALWAYS BE A SKY

POEMS SELECTED BY GEORGE SWEDE

ILLUSTRATED BY CHUM McLEOD

Nelson Canada

PUBLISHED SIMULTANEOUSLY IN 1993 BY:

Nelson Canada,
A Division of Thomson
Canada Limited
1120 Birchmount Road
Scarborough, Ontario
M1K 5G4

Houghton Mifflin Company
222 Berkeley Street
Boston, MA
02116-3764

Printed in Canada

Canadian Cataloguing in Publication Data

Main entry under title:
There will always be a sky

(Waves: language across the curriculum)

ISBN 17-604273-3

1. Children's poetry, Canadian (English).*   2. Canadian poetry (English) - 20th century.*   I. Swede, George.   II. Series.

PS8279.T54	1993	jC811'.5408'09282	C91-095375-9
PZ8.3.T54	1993		

1 2 3 4 5 6 / TRI / 9 9 8 7 6 5 4 3

DESIGN AND ART DIRECTION: Pronk&Associates

COLOUR SEPARATIONS AND FILM WORK: Colborne, Cox & Burns Inc.

Contents

Window Talk

pen meet paper
paper meet pen
write me a word
then write it again

summer flew fast
all my free days
gone like the wind
and the morning haze

pen meet paper
paper meet pen
back in my seat
at the window again

sing me a song
a musical note
dream me a dream
I just want to float

Monica Kulling

would you

i would
would you
i certainly
would
i wonder if
you would
why would
you
well
in that case
i suppose
i would
too

sean o huigin

Afternoon in March

I run
Not to anywhere,
Not away from anybody.
I run just to run,
To make my heart wham,
My eyes blur,
My side pain sharply.

I slow down at last,
Gulping the sweet air,
Almost crying …

I'm crazy.

But there was nobody ahead of me
Down that whole, long, waiting stretch of
    sun-bare sidewalk!

Oh, it was like a bird flying,
Like a song,
Like a shout!

I was freedom.

Jean Little

Toes in My Nose

I stuck my toes
In my nose
And I couldn't get them out.
It looked a little strange
And people began to shout
"Why would you ever?
My goodness — I never!"
They got in a terrible snit
It's simple, I said
As they put me to bed
I just wanted to see
If they fit.

Sheree Fitch

The Apple and the Worm

I bit an apple
    That had a worm.
I swallowed the apple,
    I swallowed the worm.
I felt it squiggle,
    I felt it squirm.
I felt it wiggle,
    I felt it turn.
It felt so slippery,
    Slimy, scummy,
I felt it land — PLOP —
    In my tummy!

I guess that worm is there to stay
Unless …
I swallow a bird some day!

Robert Heidbreder

licorice is dandy

licorice is red
or black or green
it comes in packages
or straight & clean

it comes in shoelaces
all-sorts or nibs
when the going gets tough
it sticks to my ribs

when math's a mystery
and science a stew
I plug in my licorice
and chew, chew, chew

Monica Kulling

Choices

One day I said to my friend Sam,
"Sam, just between us two,
When you grow up to age sixteen
What do you plan to do?
Sam, you could learn to play the flute
Or maybe drive a truck
Or you could run a diamond store
Or else, with any luck,
You could become an architect
Or you could be a cop
Or you could fly a super jet
Or maybe play short-stop.
You have so many choices, Sam,
You could be anything.
Please tell me what you'd *like* to be."
And Sam replied, "A king."

Gwen Molnar

Today

Today I will not live up to my potential.
Today I will not relate well to my peer group.
Today I will not contribute in class.
    I will not volunteer one thing.
Today I will not strive to do better.
Today I will not achieve or adjust or grow enriched
    or get involved.
I will not put up my hand even if the teacher is wrong
    and I can prove it.

Today I might eat the eraser off my pencil.
I'll look at clouds.
I'll be late.
I don't think I'll wash.

I need a rest.

Jean Little

I'm glad I'm adopted

For Todd and Tara

Adopted, adopted,
I'm glad I am adopted
because my mother said
"We picked you 'cause we wanted you
we loved your tiny head;
And when we took a look at you
your eyes shone like the sun
it didn't take a second
to know YOU were the one!"

Sonja Dunn

Clothes

I like new clothes.
They seem brighter, smoother, shinier.
I move carefully in them.
I remember to hang them up.
I feel taller in them — and prettier—
And I don't climb over barbed wire fences.

I like old clothes too.
I don't think about them much.
They are part of me,
Going where I go, doing whatever I feel like doing.
They are less bother and more comfortable.
They don't expect me to be so tall;
They know my size exactly.

You know, it's a funny thing ...
Friends are like clothes.

Jean Little

from "The Tonsils"

4.

I miss my tonsils. I think my throat used to feel fuller.
Now my throat feels empty a lot & maybe that's why I eat
too
fast filling the throat with as much as I can. Except food is
no
substitute for tonsils. The throat just gets empty again.

bp Nichol

Dropping
stone after
stone into
the lake

I Keep

Reappearing

George Swede

Sylvania Sputnick

Sylvania Sputnik was no normal child.
Some people said she was born to be wild.
She addled her uncle and wrangled her mother.
She frazzled her friends and fandango'd her brother.
She loved getting dirty and grousing and griping,
And drove people nuts, which was very exciting.
She might have got better if she'd tried to, I guess,
But Sylvania Sputnick just couldn't care less.

Charles Wilkins

Dickery Dean

"What's the matter
    With Dickery Dean?
He jumped right into
    The washing machine!"

"Nothing's the matter
    With Dickery Dean —
He dove in dirty,
    And he jumped out clean!"

Dennis Lee

Where It's At

We have hopscotch on the sidewalk,
We have neighbors' dogs and cats,
We have market stalls and soccer balls
And skates and baseball bats.

We have ice-cream carts in summer,
We have chestnuts in the fall,
We have soft-drink stands and city bands,
And that's not nearly all!

We have downtown parks to play in,
We have long parades of bikes,
We have swimming pools and summer schools,
And gangs of kids on trikes.

We can't all live in the city
(Think how crowded it would be!)
But for summer fun, from sun to sun,
It's *the* place for Sam and me!

Gwen Molnar

my grandmother

my grandmother's nearly blind

she counts change by the window
to order a loaf of bread
before the store closes

she finds enough sunshine
to tell a penny
from a dime

LeRoy Gorman

Hear the Drum Speak

Hear the Drum speak.
Let it remind you
of days with the Old Woman,
the Visions she saw
the Dreams she had.

Hear the Drum speak
of days of learning
to smoke the Pipe
of burning Tobacco
and Sweetgrass.

Hear the Drum speak
of days we Fasted
for guidance
from the Creator
and in gratitude.

Hear the Drum speak …

Sky Blue Mary Morin

Broken Day

I don't care
how high the clouds are,
how white they curdle
in the whey of the sky,
or if the sun
is kind to the flowers,
or why the wind
plays at storms in the trees:

the robin hiding
in the garden bushes
has a broken wing.

Raymond Souster

Jacks

Seven geese in the sky
changing formation
the way jacks fall
five and two
four and three
your fingers scooping them
deftly off the table top.

Joy Kogawa

back & forth

two
track
&
in
outside
if
will
(not
that's
their
it's
back
forth
I
while
news
TV
bleak
two
talking
peace
building

rabbits
back
forth
snow
wondering
spring
come
really)
not
worry
mine
&
inside
pace
the
on
is
about
sides
about
while
bombs

LeRoy Gorman

Prayer of the Mystic Warrior

Oh great mystery
And man above,
Hear me now
For I stand before you
Humble and obedient.
Make me strong
To fight my enemies.
Give me strength
To protect my loved ones.
Help me
Overcome my weaknesses.

Make

Me

Worthy

Wayne Keon

Sun-dance

You can hear the drums
You can hear the chants
You can hear the rattles
You can hear the flutes

You can see children playing
You can see people laughing
You can see tents in a circle
You can see the sacred lodge in the centre

You can hear the crier
You can see the colourful offerings up around the lodge
You can smell the sweetgrass burning
You can feel the warmth of the sacred fire burning

You can see the dancers in rhythm with the drum beat
You can see the servers inside the lodge
You can see families with their giveaways enter the sacred
lodge
You can hear their thanksgivings and prayers

You can hear the singers on horseback
As they sing in unison around the lodge
You can see young and old, sit and watch
You can feel the spirit of our forefathers

Ah! The Sun-dance — the most sacred of our ceremonies
It has been practised for years
It must be carried on for more
Because it is so

Gayle Weenie

35

After coming
all that way

Sunbeam rests
on the couch

George Swede

; ;

Paw marks
in the snow ; ;
           ; ;
         ; ;
       ; ;
     ; ;
    ; ;
   ; ;
  ; ;
  ; ;
semi; ; colons
   ; ;
   ; ;
punctuate
the cat' ' ' ' ' ' ' ' ' 's trail
to my window, , , , , , , , , ,
where he claws
exclamat!on marks
on the frosted glass! ! ! ! ! ! ! ! ! ! !

Ted Plantos

Arctic Fox

White as the white of snow on snow,
He curls in the whirls of the arctic blow;
We can't see him sleep and can't see him go —
White as the white of snow on snow.

Ellen Obed

Angels

I'm making angels here in the snow;
The temperature's minus twenty-seven;
If I don't stop doing it pretty darn soon
I'll be flapping my wings in heaven.

Lois Simmie

All

of

win

ter

in

this

one

long

ici

cle

George Swede

Lotsa Winds

How many sounds
do the four winds make?

Hundreds and hundreds
for goodness' sake

Listen listen
to the sound
As they whoosh
around and 'round

Misssssssssssssstral
SSSSSSSSSSSSSSSirroco
ChChChChChChChChChChinoooooooook
Monssoooooooooooooooooooooon
Doldruuuuuuuuuuuuuuuuum
Traaaaaaaaaaaade wiiiiiiind
Northsouthwesteast wiiiiiiiinds
ZZZZZZZZZZZZZZZZZZZephyr

If you make these sounds again
You may start a HURRICANE!

Sonja Dunn

Windsong

My People talk to the winds …
Winds of the four seasons;
And voices of the winds come back.
The West wind like moccasins in the grass,
East wind a rain-drenched crying child
Lost in the canyons of a Pass.
A strong man, Giant of the North,
Drums big talk, fierce, and wild,
But South wind, soft from over the hill
Chinook, chinook, tender and mild
Sings a sage-brush lullaby …
  Windsong of my People.

Leonora Hayden-McDowell

As Far

As far as
the eye
can see

and as
far as
the sea
can eye

there will
always be
a sky

George Swede

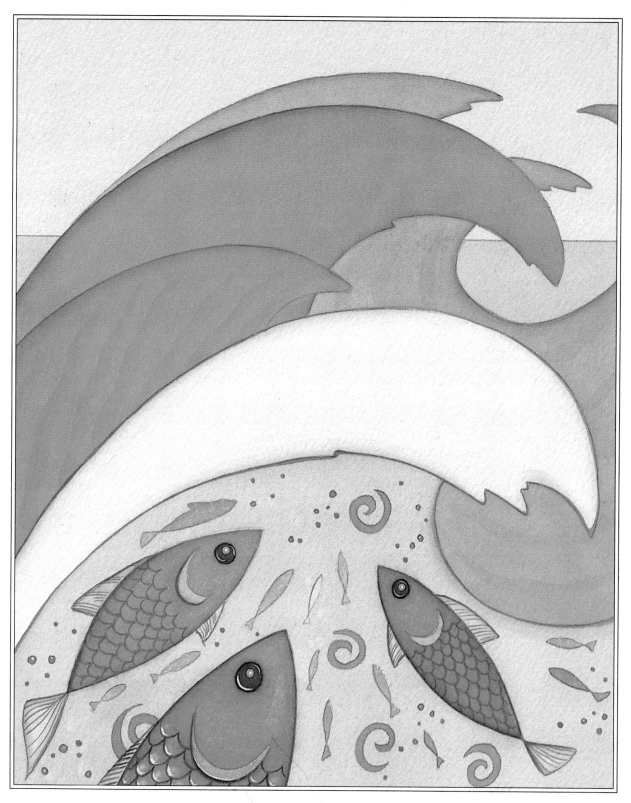

Acknowledgements

For each of the selections listed below, grateful acknowledgement is made for permission to reprint original or copyrighted material, as follows:

Window Talk by Monica Kulling. Reprinted by permission of the author.

would you by sean o huigin. Reprinted by permission of Black Moss Press.

Afternoon in March from: **Hey World, Here I Am!** Text copyright © 1986 by Jean Little. Reprinted by permission of Kids Can Press Ltd., Toronto, Canada. Reprinted by permission of HarperCollins Publishers.

Toes in My Nose by Sheree Fitch: from Toes in My Nose and Other Poems, published by Doubleday Canada Limited. © 1987 by Sheree Fitch.

The Apple and the Worm: from *Don't Eat Spiders*, poems © Robert Heidbreder 1985; reprinted by permission of Oxford University Press Canada.

licorice is dandy by Monica Kulling. Reprinted by permission of the author.

Choices: Text © 1987 by Gwen Molnar. Reprinted by permission of Scholastic Canada Ltd.

Today: TEXT from HEY WORLD, HERE I AM! by JEAN LITTLE. TEXT COPYRIGHT © 1986 by JEAN LITTLE. Reprinted by permission of HarperCollins Publishers.

I'm glad I'm adopted: © Sonja Dunn from **Crackers & Crumbs *(or Butterscotch Dreams)***. Published by Pembroke Publishers Limited, 528 Hood Road, Markham, Ontario L3R 3K9. Reprinted with permission.

Clothes: TEXT from HEY WORLD, HERE I AM! by JEAN LITTLE. TEXT COPYRIGHT © 1986 by JEAN LITTLE. Reprinted by permission of HarperCollins Publishers.

from "The Tonsils" by bp Nichol. Reprinted by permission of Black Moss Press.

"Dropping": from *High Wire Spider* by George Swede. Published by Three Trees Press. Reprinted by permission of the author.

Sylvania Sputnick: From *Old Mrs Schmatterbung and Other Friends* by Charles Wilkins. Used by permission of the Canadian Publishers, McClelland & Stewart, Toronto.

Dickery Dean by Dennis Lee: from *Jelly Belly*, published by Macmillan of Canada, © 1983, Dennis Lee.

Where It's At: Text © copyright 1987 by Gwen Molnar. Reprinted by permission of Scholastic Canada Ltd.

my grandmother by LeRoy Gorman: from *dandelions & dreams* (Moonstone Press).

Hear the Drum Speak by Sky Blue Mary Morin: from *Writing the Circle*. Copyright © 1990. Reprinted by permission of the author.

Broken Day: reprinted from *Collected Poems of Raymond Souster* by permission of Oberon Press.

Jacks by Joy Kogawa: Published with the permission of Mosaic Press, from *Woman in the Woods*, Mosaic Press, Oakville, Ontario, 1985.

back & forth by LeRoy Gorman: from *dandelions & dreams* (Moonstone Press).

Prayer of the Mystic Warrior: from *Sweetgrass II* by Wayne Keon. Reprinted by permission of the author.

Sun-dance by Gayle Weenie: from *Writing the Circle*. Copyright © 1990. Reprinted by permission of the author.

"After coming": from *Leaping Lizard* by George Swede. Published by Three Trees Press. Reprinted by permission of the author.

"Paw marks": Copyright © 1990 by Ted Plantos, from *The Universe Is One Poem*, published by Simon & Pierre Publishing Co. Ltd. Used by permission.

Arctic Fox: from *Wind in My Pocket*. Published by Breakwater, St. John's, Newfoundland. © Copyright Ellen Bryan Obed.

Angels: from *Who Greased the Shoelaces?* by Lois Simmie. Reproduced with the permission of Stoddart Publishing Co. Limited, 34 Lesmill Rd., Don Mills, Ontario, Canada.

"All": from *Time Is Flies* by George Swede. Published by Three Trees Press. Reprinted by permission of the author.

Lotsa Winds: © Sonja Dunn from **Crackers & Crumbs *(or Butterscotch Dreams)***. Published by Pembroke Publishers Limited, 528 Hood Road, Markham, Ontario L3R 3K9. Reprinted with permission.

Windsong by Leonora Hayden-McDowell: from *Writing the Circle*. Copyright © 1990. Reprinted by permission of the author.

As Far: from *High Wire Spider* by George Swede. Published by Three Trees Press. Reprinted by permission of the author.